Grade 2

The Syllabus of Examinations should be read for details of requirements, especially those for scales, aural tests and sight-reading. Attention should be paid to the Special Notices on the front inside cover, where warning is given of changes.

The syllabus is obtainable from music dealers or from The Associated Board of the Royal Schools of Music, 14 Bedford Square, London WC1B 3JG (please send stamped addressed envelope measuring about 9×6 ins.).

In overseas centres, information may be obtained from the Local Representative or Resident Secretary.

REQUIREMENTS

SCALES AND BROKEN CHORDS (from memory)

Scales
major and minor (melodic or harmonic at candidate's choice): each hand separately, and hands together in similar motion one octave apart in the following keys:
C, G, D, A, E, F majors (two octaves);
A, E, D minors (one octave or two at candidate's choice);
and in contrary motion with both hands beginning and ending on the key-note (unison), in the key of C major (two octaves).

Chromatic Scale
beginning on D, with each hand separately (one octave).

Broken Chords
formed from the chords of C, G & F major, and A, E & D minor, with each hand separately, according to the example shown in the syllabus.

PLAYING AT SIGHT (see current syllabus)

AURAL TESTS (see current syllabus)

THREE PIECES

Candidates must prepare Nos.1 & 2 from the *same* list, A or B, but may choose No.3 from *either* list or one of the further alternatives listed below:

Fibich   Morning Pastimes
Maikapar   The Moth
These are included in More Romantic Pieces for Piano, Book I, *published by the Associated Board*

Editor for the Associated Board: **Lionel Salter**

A:1
STUDY in C

LE COUPPEY, Op.24 No.10

Scarcely had Felix Le Couppey completed his studies at the Paris Conservatoire at the age of 17 than he was taken on to its staff. He was to remain there for the rest of his life, becoming a busy teacher and composer of a great quantity of music. The phrasing and dynamics here are editorial.   L.S.

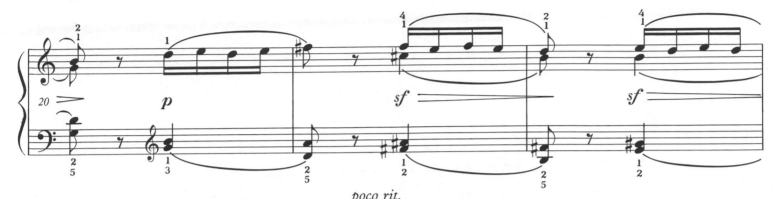

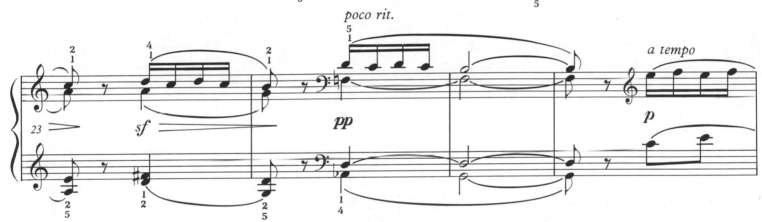

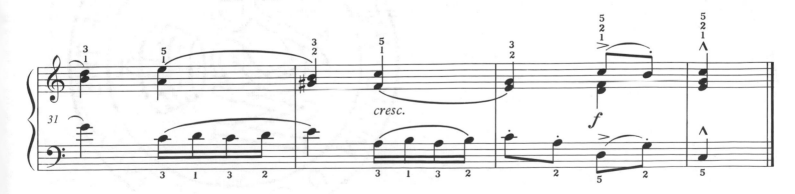

A:2
SCHERZO in F

Edited by
Howard Ferguson

HÄSSLER, Op.38 No.49

Source: *Cinquante Pièces à l'usage des commençans*, published in Moscow, where Hässler spent over a quarter of a century after two years in London as a successful performer and teacher, and a year as court pianist to the Grand Duke Alexander in St Petersburg. Candidates with small hands may omit the notes in brackets in bars 7 and 8.   L.S.

A:3
LITTLE SONG

KABALEVSKY, Op.27 No.2

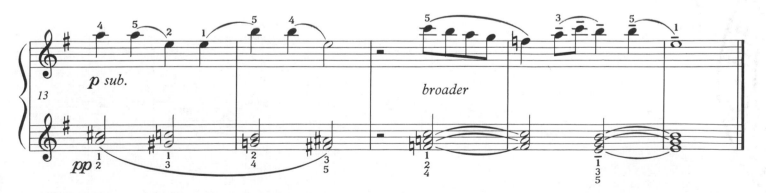

Although he has to his credit five operas, four symphonies and six concertos (three of them for young players), Kabalevsky is best known for his work in the educational field. After being appointed a professor at the Moscow Conservatory, he became head of a commission on the musical education of children and, later, president of the International Society for Musical Education. L.S.

AB 2305

B:1
LESSON in C

HOOK, Op.81 No.4

Source: *New Guida di Musica*, London c.1796. James Hook, born in Norwich, was precociously gifted (playing concerts at the age of 6) and became enormously popular as organist and composer first at Marylebone Gardens and then at Vauxhall, where he wrote more than 2,000 songs, including the well-known 'Lass of Richmond Hill'. The phrasing, articulation and dynamics here are editorial.   L.S.

B:2
SAD AT HEART

The Austrian composer Robert Fuchs, the first of whose five symphonies was admired by Brahms, was a distinguished teacher of composition whose pupils included Mahler, Sibelius and Hugo Wolf. The present piece comes from his *Jugend-album* (Children's album), published in Berlin in 1890.   L.S.

B:3
THREE BLUE MICE
from 'Swinging Rhymes'

TERENCE GREAVES

Steady, with a firm beat ♩ = c.120

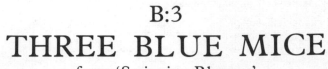

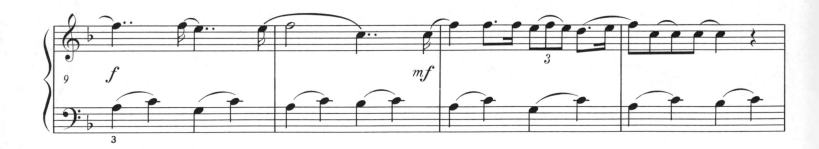

AB 2305

Printed in England by Headley Brothers Ltd The Invicta Press Ashford Kent and London